2.95

DATE DUE

FEB 0 8 2006	
MAR 1 1 2006	
MAY 0 1 2006	
MAY 2 6 2006	

GAYLORD   PRINTED IN U.S.A.

Days That Changed The World

THE
SEPTEMBER 11TH
TERRORIST ATTACKS

Fiona Macdonald

WORLD ALMANAC® LIBRARY

Please visit our web site at: www.worldalmanaclibrary.com
For a free color catalog describing World Almanac® Library's
list of high-quality books and multimedia programs,
call 1-800-848-2928 (USA) or 1-800-387-3178 (Canada).
World Almanac® Library's fax: (414) 332-3567.

Library of Congress Cataloging-in-Publication Data available upon request from publisher.
Fax (414) 336-0157 for the attention of the Publishing Records Department.

ISBN 0-8368-5572-8 (lib. bdg.)
ISBN 0-8368-5579-5 (softcover)

This North American edition first published in 2004 by
World Almanac® Library
330 West Olive Street, Suite 100
Milwaukee, WI 53212 USA

This U.S. edition copyright © 2004 by World Almanac® Library. Original edition copyright © 2003 by ticktock
Entertainment Ltd. First published in Great Britain in 2003 by ticktock Media Ltd., Unit 2, Orchard Business
Centre, North Farm Road, Tunbridge Wells, Kent TN2 3XF. Additional end matter copyright © 2004 by
World Almanac® Library.

We would like to thank: Tall Tree Ltd, Lizzy Bacon, and Ed Simkins for their assistance.

World Almanac® Library editor: Carol Ryback
World Almanac® Library cover design: Steve Schraenkler

Photo Credits:
t=top, b=bottom, c=center, l=left, r=right, OFC=outside front cover
Alamy: 1, 6bl, 10tl, 19tl, 29tr, 35t, 42cl. Aviation Images: 5tl, 28b. CORBIS: 4t, 7, 9b, 10-11, 12-13c, 13c, 14, 15c, 16-17, 18-19, 20, 21, 23, 29c, 42tr, 42b, 43cl.
Creatas: 5b, 19tl, 25, 26b, 27 (both), 28t, 30, 31, 32, 33, 34, 36, 37t, 38t, 38-39. NORAD: 22b. PA Photos: 22tr, 24t & 43t, 39r, 40-41, 40tl, 41tr, 43r.

Every effort has been made to trace the copyright holders, and we apologize in advance for any
unintentional omissions. We would be pleased to insert the appropriate acknowledgments in any
subsequent edition of this publication.

Printed in Hong Kong

1 2 3 4 5 6 7 8 9 08 07 06 05 04

CONTENTS

INTRODUCTION

Flames engulf the south tower (left) of the World Trade Center as United Airlines Flight 175 hits its target. About fifteen minutes earlier, American Airlines Flight 11 rammed into the north tower.

The American flag serves as a proud symbol of freedom around the world. The events of September 11, 2001, made many Americans consider how others viewed their country.

Tuesday, September 11, 2001 has been called the "Attack on America." It was the day when more than five thousand people — mostly U.S. citizens — were killed or injured while peacefully going about their everyday business. It was the world's worst single terrorist act and the first major terrorist attack on U.S. soil.

The four aircraft hijacked that morning became gigantic airborne weapons as the terrorists deliberately crashed into their respective targets. Two planes hit the twin towers of the World Trade Center in New York City and one plane smashed into the Pentagon (the U.S. Defense Department's headquarters just outside of Washington, D.C.). It's believed that passengers aboard the fourth plane fought against the hijackers, thwarting their plans and causing the plane to plow into an open field in southwestern Pennsylvania. Everyone aboard the planes died, as did thousands of others. The attacks killed citizens of many nations. Most of the victims were unknown to the terrorists and just happened to work in or were visiting the buildings that the planes hit. Hundreds of police officers, firefighters, and members of ambulance and rescue teams also died — not from the plane crashes themselves, but when the World Trade Center towers collapsed on them. Millions watched in horror as television news crews beamed live coverage of the collapsing towers.

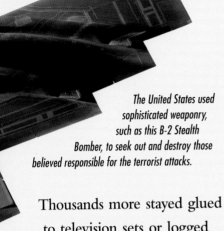

The United States used sophisticated weaponry, such as this B-2 Stealth Bomber, to seek out and destroy those believed responsible for the terrorist attacks.

States, a country not used to living with the threat of potential terrorist attacks. September 11 profoundly altered Americans' view of themselves, their country, and the world. Events that day also changed the pattern of international relationships forever. Why had this happened — and who was behind it?

Thousands more stayed glued to television sets or logged on to the Internet as events of the day unfolded in New York City, at the Pentagon, and in Pennsylvania. All of these observers were powerless to help but too stunned to turn away from their screens. This was not a disaster movie with computer-generated special effects. It was real life and it was terrible. The attacks created a new sense of fear, bewilderment, and uncertainty in the United

Attention focused on the Middle East, a region south and east of the Mediterranean Sea. Many religious and

An exhausted New York firefighter reflects on the events of the day.

INTRODUCTION

Secretary General Kofi Annan heads the United Nations (UN). Some UN members disagreed with the reasons behind the United States's 2003 invasion of Iraq.

After the United States toppled the Taliban regime in Afghanistan, it turned its attention to Iraq. The U.S. government based its invasion of Iraq in part on the belief that Iraqi leader Saddam Hussein may have played a part in the September 11 attacks.

secular leaders and members of the general population in this area disagreed with the United States's involvement in the Middle East, especially its support for Israel. They felt that the United States was helping Israel suppress the establishment of a Palestinian nation. Resentment against Western economic, social, and cultural influence in the region grew. Terrorist groups, often based on an extreme interpretation of Islam, formed. At first, terrorists concentrated on attacking targets in the Middle East. Over the past thirty years, these extremists began selecting targets around the globe, hoping to increase exposure for their cause.

As peaceful nations looked for someone to hold responsible for the September 11 attacks, governments made new allies and turned against former friends. Groups and leaders formerly funded and supported by the U.S. government were now viewed as enemies. These included Osama bin Laden, whom the United States had supported in his fight against the Soviet presence in Afghanistan; and Saddam Hussein, the leader of Iraq, whom the U.S. had supported in his war against Iran.

Clearly, the United States's old way of doing things had changed. The United States felt justified in attacking these groups, including other countries' governments, and refused to sit back and wait for another terrorist attack while the international community decided what to do next.

Consequently, the United States adopted a new, tougher role for itself as it hunted for those believed responsible for the deadly attacks.

found itself caught between calls for action against terrorism and urges of restraint against breaking international laws.

The September 11 terrorist attacks provoked debate and discussion far beyond the borders of the United States. Britain's prime minister Tony Blair summed up the situation: "This is not a battle between the United States and terrorism, but between the free and democratic world and terrorism." Meanwhile, the United Nations, an international peacekeeping organization with headquarters in New York City,

Osama bin Laden founded and funded al-Qaeda — the terrorist group responsible for the attacks of September 11, 2001.

CULTURAL COLLISIONS

Nothing illustrates the global spread of U.S. commercial influence better than Coca-Cola. Consumers all over the world recognize its distinct logo — which has been translated into several different languages and alphabets.

For nearly fifty years after the end of World War II, the world's two most powerful nations, the United States and the Soviet Union, were enemies with different ways of life and different political ideals. The U.S. was a free-market democracy, while communism ruled the Soviet Union. The two superpowers mistrusted and misunderstood each other and their leaders quarreled publicly as both countries worked to spread their influence around the globe. Although the U.S. and the Soviet Union never fought each other directly, the strong tensions between them became known as the "Cold War."

Alone — and powerful

By the 1980s, the Soviet Union's economy was so weak that the country could no longer afford its military, political, and economic rivalry with the United States. Perhaps more importantly, the people's appetite for communism in both the Soviet Union and Eastern Europe was also waning, and by the end of the decade, a succession of countries had removed their communist leaders from power. In December 1991, the communist government in the Soviet Union itself disbanded and the Soviet Union broke up. This left the United States as the world's only remaining superpower.

CAPITALISM

Capitalism is a "free market" economic system in which the means of producing wealth, such as factories and shops, are owned by private individuals ("entrepreneurs") or corporations. In a capitalistic system, anyone can set up a business — if they have the money — and grow rich if it makes a profit. Businesses compete with one another freely, with relatively little government interference. Supply and demand control free-market economies. Taxes are relatively low, and government rules and welfare benefits are kept to a minimum. Risks for entrepreneurs starting a business are high. If they fail, they might lose their home or suffer other financial consequences; if they succeed, they could become very rich.

From cola to computers

U.S. citizens enjoy one of the highest standards of living in the world. For most of the 1990s, the U.S. economy was booming. From Australia to Zimbabwe, "American" products and icons — from soft drinks and food to clothing to movie stars and music — were in demand all over the world. Advances in U.S. technology, especially computer software and the Internet, revolutionized global communications and influenced the style and content of news and entertainment media almost everywhere.

Georg

A takeover?

Many people in many countries admired the energy and enterprise of the United States. It had become the richest, most powerful country in the world. U.S. technology and culture seemed to dominate international affairs. Some people watched in dismay, fearing that products, movies, sports, fashions, and foods from the world's only superpower were threatening to replace local, ethnic, and religious cultures and traditions. Anger rose as

these insecurities increased. Certain groups wanted to rebel against what they saw as "American" values being imposed on them without their choice. Some of these rebel groups believed that the U.S. was becoming too powerful, arrogant, and insensitive to the concerns of the rest of the world.

A crowd waves tiny U.S. flags during a political rally.

U.S. President George W. Bush became more involved in world affairs after the September 11 terrorist attacks.

'The American destiny is what our fathers dreamed, a land of the free, and the home of the brave; but only the brave can be free. Science has made the dream of today's reality for all the earth if we have the courage and vision to build it. American democracy must furnish the engineers of world plenty — the builders of world peace and freedom.'

American writer Marian Le Sueur (1877–1954)

CULTURAL COLLISIONS

Wall Street (above) is the financial center of the United States. Its name signifies economic power and wealth.

Money talks!

The U.S. is home to many multinational companies, such as McDonald's and Coca Cola, which sell their products and extend their operations all over the world. These companies take advantage of the free-market system, often locating their factories in countries where wages are low in order to produce goods as cheaply as possible, and then selling the products in wealthier nations at prices high enough to cover costs and reap a profit. Supporters of free trade claim that the system helps poor countries develop their economies, creates jobs, and improves standards of living. Although a newly reorganized international economic "watchdog," the World Trade Organization (WTO) located in Geneva, Switzerland, officially began overseeing trade and settling trade disputes between countries on January 1, 1995, critics argue that free trade exploits workers in poorer countries by taking advantage of their powerlessness and that the free-trade system forces all countries to adopt materialistic beliefs and values.

FOUR *freedoms*

In 1941, American President Franklin D. Roosevelt proclaimed that, in his view, all people — no matter their country — are entitled to the "Four Freedoms," already enjoyed by United States citizens. The freedoms are:

- *Freedom of Speech and Expression*
- *Freedom of Worship*
- *Freedom from Want*
- *Freedom from Fear*

Religious freedom

The United States not only supports free trade, but also proclaims other freedoms it believes all people should enjoy. These include free speech — the right to express opinions without fear of punishment — and freedom of religion. Although many Americans are deeply religious, the U.S. is a secular (non-religious) country by law. The right to hold any religious faith — or none — is guaranteed by the Bill of Rights section of the U.S. Constitution. Approved in 1791, the Bill of Rights lists the first ten amendments to the Constitution — which was approved in 1787.

The American way

While Americans often criticize their national and local governments, most believe that these freedoms make their country the best in the world. Millions of immigrants who flocked to the United States in the nineteenth and twentieth centuries to seek a better future were proud to follow the "American way" of life. Most Americans hold dear their guaranteed freedoms and democratic principles; they admire their nation's economic strength and military power; and they respect national symbols such as the American flag.

Disapproval

While the American ideals of freedom and democracy are shared by many citizens of Western Europe and in countries that had once been under communist control, these ideals did not please everybody. Some powerful nations, including China, admired economic freedom but did not support the same level of civil freedom. Many Muslim nations, including Saudi Arabia and Iran, feared that Western ways would corrupt their society and change their traditions. By the late twentieth century, the dislike of Western society in many parts of the Muslim world mingled with ancient religious and political tensions to create an explosive mixture of fear and distrust.

"The Westerners have lost the vision of heaven,

All they care about is food and possessions,

But the pure soul is untouched by greed and desire.

Communism is only concerned with physical needs...

It is based on equality of greed...

But true brotherhood belongs to the heart,

It does not need material things."

Taken from "Javidnama," written by Muslim poet Muhammad Iqbal in 1932

"Liberty Enlightening the World," commonly known as the Statue of Liberty, greets citizens, visitors, and immigrants arriving in New York Harbor.

CULTURAL COLLISIONS

LEBANON

GOLAN
HEIGHTS

SYRIA

MEDITERRANEAN
SEA

WEST
BANK

DEAD
SEA

GAZA
STRIP

ISRAEL

JORDAN

EGYPT

Disputes continue between Israelis and Palestinians over control of the West Bank and the Gaza Strip.

The Middle East

The section of the Middle East often called the "Holy Land" is divided among Syria, Israel, Jordan, and the disputed Palestinian territories. The Holy Land is sacred to people from three of the world's great religions: Christianity, Judaism, and Islam. Followers of all of these faiths often visit holy sites in Jerusalem — the most important city in the Holy Land.

"Promised Land"

The "Promised Land" for Jews is where their ancestors settled after Moses led them out of Egypt in about 1200 B.C. They believe the land was promised to them by God. The same area is sacred to Christians because Jesus Christ lived and preached there. They believe that Christ rose from the dead after his crucifixion in about A.D. 30.

God's last messenger

Muslims honor Moses and Jesus Christ as prophets — messengers sent by God to show people the right way to live. They believe that the Prophet Muhammad, who lived from A.D. 570–632, was God's greatest — and last — messenger. Like Jews and Christians, Muslims respect the land where Moses and Jesus once preached. Muslims also feel special reverence for the Arabian holy cities of Mecca, where the Prophet Muhammad spent most of his life, and Medina, where he is buried. They also honor other holy places in neighboring Middle Eastern countries, including Iraq and Iran.

THE DOME *of the* Rock

The Dome of the Rock in Jerusalem that was built about A.D. 691. It is considered a holy site by both Muslims, who call it the Noble Sanctuary, and Jews, who call it Temple Mount. Followers of Muslim believe that the Prophet Muhammad made a miraculous journey to heaven from a rocky outcrop here and returned to teach people how to pray. Jews believe God commanded Abraham to sacrifice his son Isaac at the Dome. It was also the place where the Jewish King Solomon built the first great Jewish temple to worship God.

Disputed territory

The Holy Land has always been disputed territory. In ancient times, it was home to several warring peoples including Jews, Philistines, and Samaritans. It was conquered by the Romans in A.D. 6, and by Muslims in A.D. 634. During the Crusades from 1098 until 1197, Christian soldiers ruled the Holy Land. Muslim armies took control back from the Christians, and the area became part of the Muslim Ottoman Empire in 1516. They ruled it, along with most of the Arabian Peninsula and Iraq, until 1917 — when the Ottoman Empire's power collapsed after it was defeated in World War I. Since then, many parts of the Middle East, including the Holy Land, have been constantly threatened by upheaval or war.

Sand and oil

As well as being "holy," the lands of the Middle East are remarkable in another way. In the early nineteenth century, geologists first discovered vast reserves of oil deep beneath the stony desert sands. By the late twentieth century,

the Middle East's oil industry was booming. More than two-thirds of all the world's known oil deposits belong to Iran, Iraq, Saudi Arabia, Kuwait, and neighboring smaller countries. Although this oil wealth gives Middle Eastern countries enormous power, it makes them vulnerable to attack.

This Saudi refinery processes Persian Gulf oil. Wealth from oil has transformed a previously impoverished area into a region of wealthy, high-tech kingdoms.

BLACK *gold*

Oil, often called "black gold," is an extraordinarily valuable commodity. It is considered a nonrenewable source, which means that once current supplies are exhausted, people cannot create more. A complete cutoff of oil supplies would paralyze everyday life in all industrialized nations. Cars, aircraft, trains, power-supply systems and many other machines all rely on oil-based fuels. Many plastics, detergents, cosmetics, dyes, food flavorings, textiles, and lubricants are also made from oil.

CULTURAL COLLISIONS

An Afghan mujahedin (Muslim guerrilla fighter) defends his territory after the Soviet Union invaded Afghanistan in 1979.

Independence

In 1920, after the collapse of the Ottoman Empire, an organization called the League of Nations gave Britain and France special authority to govern large areas of the Middle East. Many Middle Eastern peoples instead demanded the right to become independent nations. They wanted to govern themselves and set their own laws that were often based on religious beliefs.

Saudi Arabia

Abd al-Aziz Ibn Saud (1880–1953) led the demand for independence in Arabia. He supported the strict Wahhabi religious reform movement, which aimed to purify Islam. With the help of Wahhabi brotherhoods, Saud helped make Arabia an independent nation in 1932. Ibn Saud became king and declared that Arabia should be ruled according to *shariyah* (Muslim holy law, based on the Muslim holy book, the al-Qur'an), and by royal decree. He also renamed the state after his family. After oil was discovered in Saudi Arabia in the 1930s, Ibn Saud became even more powerful.

Iraq and Iran

Neighboring Iraq and Iran, which also had rich reserves of oil, won independence in 1921 and 1925, respectively. For many years afterward, however, European and U.S. governments interfered in politics in this region, backing some leaders while working to weaken others. Western oil companies did not want to lose control of profitable oil reserves and refineries, and Western governments wanted to stop other powerful nations from controlling Middle Eastern oil. In 1979, anti-Western Muslim leaders seized power in Iran, launching a strict "Islamic Revolution."

Israel

Jewish people also demanded a homeland of their own. The First Zionist Congress (international meeting of Jews) was held in 1897. In 1917, British Foreign Secretary Arthur Balfour issued a statement supporting a new Jewish country in Palestine, so long as "nothing shall be done which may prejudice the civil and religious rites of existing non-Jewish communities." By 1939, half

The CRUSADES

The Crusades were a series of seven wars fought to win control of the Holy Land between the eleventh and fourteenth centuries. Preachers who feared that Islam would soon spread westward into Europe inspired the Crusaders (knights and foot soldiers) to continue in battle. Soldiers from many Muslim lands, from Turkey to Egypt, fought to defend their Islamic faith and their Muslim lifestyle and laws. Brutal fighting and atrocities committed by Christians and Muslims created an enduring heritage of bitterness and misunderstanding.

"PURE" *Islam*

Arab religious reformer Muhammad Ibn Abd al-Wahhab (died 1791) believed that certain Muslim customs that were adopted over the centuries — such as honoring saints at shrines — were damaging to Islam. He also condemned Western ideas and values. Al-Wahhab called for a return to very strict "pure," Muslim belief and worship that focused on "tawhid," the unity and oneness of God. Wahhabi ideas helped establish the Kingdom of Saudi Arabia and serve as a guide to its government's policies.

a million Jewish people had settled in Palestine, and there were serious tensions between Arabs (both Christian and Muslim) and Jews. In 1947, the UN divided Palestine into Jewish and Arab states, and the nation of Israel was born. Israel has a Western-style secular constitution, but Jewish religious laws and traditions play an important role in shaping its citizens' lives.

Holy laws, holy wars

Variations in religious laws often make conflicts worse when neighboring countries of different faiths become involved in a dispute. Ever since the Crusades, soldiers from different faiths justified many appalling acts of violence committed in the Middle East by claiming that they were fighting a "holy war." When all conflicting parties believe that only their religious cause has Divine blessing, they feel free to indulge their hatred, prejudice, and intolerance towards others of different faiths. This sentiment often inflames seemingly minor differences between cultures, traditions, or methods of government and can also affect attitudes regarding people of different races.

Radical Muslims in Pakistan carry images of their hero Osama bin Laden after the September 11 attacks. Pakistan's secular government often finds itself caught between its Western allies and interests and many of its fundamentalist Muslim citizens.

Terrorism has a long history. The word was first used in 1793, during a period of the French Revolution that became known as "The Terror." At that time, republicans with extreme views used guillotines to execute the French king and queen, as well as thousands of members of the French nobility and people who were suspected of sympathizing with them. Terrorist attacks are still common in many parts of the world. Typical terror tactics include assassination, hostage-taking, hijacking, and mass-murder.

Kenya's Kikuyu people have always been among the poorest in that country. In the 1950s, the Mau Mau organization, which included extreme members of the Kikuyu, launched a series of attacks aimed at forcing the European settlers out of Kenya.

Bombs and bullets

In Russia during the 1870s and 1880s, a radical group known as "*Narodnaya Volya*" ("The People's Will") threw bombs at members of the Russian government, and shot dead the Russian monarch Czar Alexander II in 1881. They hoped that once the hated leaders were overthrown, ordinary people would revolt and create a new communist state.

Surprise attacks

In 1950s Kenya, the secret Mau Mau organization was formed by radical members of the Kikuyu people to fight against Europeans who had settled in their country. They made nighttime attacks on remote villages and farms. Later, the Mau Mau became anti-Christian as well as anti-European, and very violent. They killed more than eleven thousand Africans and fifty Europeans. As a result of Mau Mau activities, many Europeans left Kenya when the nation became independent from Britain in 1963.

WHO *is a terrorist?*

Some experts say that terrorists are people who use terror to get what they want, even if they have good reasons to justify their actions. Other experts argue that people who normally campaign by peaceful, lawful means may occasionally use terror to fight for their rights or to defend themselves from powerful enemies. Their behavior is terrible and terrifying, but it does not make them terrorists.

Suicide bombers

In Sri Lanka during the 1970s, members of the Tamil ethnic minority protested against their treatment by the majority Sinhalese, and demanded an independent Tamil homeland in northern Sri Lanka. While many worked peacefully, others established camps to train terrorists known as the "Tamil Tigers." Suicide bombers were sent to buses, trains, shops and market places. They aimed to kill the maximum number of people, including women and children. This tactic caused widespread panic.

Hijacking and publicity

In the Middle East in the 1970s, Palestinian terrorists hijacked several aircraft. The hijackers set the unharmed passengers free, then blew the planes up on the ground. The terrorists wanted maximum publicity for their cause — an end to the Israeli occupation of the West Bank area, and the establishment of an independent Palestinian state. In 1976, Muslim leader Sheik Yassin Ahmad founded Hamas, a Palestinian resistance movement. It was originally nonmilitant, but soon began using increasingly violent means, including suicide bombings and assassinations.

Members of Hamas often hide their identity. "Hamas" stands for haraka musallaha islamya, or Islamic Armed Movement.

> "Millions of innocent children are being killed as I speak. They are being killed in Iraq without committing any sins… In these days, Israeli tanks infest Palestine… and we don't hear anyone raising his voice or moving a limb."
>
> **Osama bin Laden**
> prior to the
> U.S. terrorist attacks

STRUGGLE AND CHANGE

Basque Region

(above) The Basque live in the western Pyrenees Mountains between France and Spain.

Worldwide terrorism

Terrorism is not like ordinary warfare. Terrorist fighters are not recruited, trained, or commanded by lawful governments. They do not obey any of the normal "rules of war" agreed upon by governments to protect innocent civilians, prisoners of war, and medical teams on both sides. Terrorist groups operate all over the world in many different countries.

Freedom fighters

The Basque — an ethnic minority with a unique culture — live in the western Pyrenees Mountains between France and Spain. In the 1990s, a group known as ETA (the Basque Freedom and Liberty organization) recruited members from the Basque area. ETA used car bombings and murders to terrorize cities and towns. It claimed to be fighting for freedom and for right to form a separate Basque state. ETA claimed that violence was necessary to make the Spanish and French governments listen to its demands.

The region known as Northern Ireland is part of the United Kingdom. The independent Republic of Ireland lies to the south.

Mighty enemies

Also in the 1990s, in Chechnya, a region in the southwest Russian Federation, rebels demanded independence from Russia. The rebels realized that although they could not win a traditional war against Russia, the use of terrorist tactics known as guerrilla warfare, would at least achieve maximum impact for even a small number of terrorists fighters with weapons. Russian resistance to Chechnya's independence has only increased the determination of the Chechen rebels, despite much suffering on both sides.

A masked terrorist throws a Molotov cocktail in West Belfast, Northern Ireland. The situation in the Irish province is complicated by a religious divide as well as a political one.

Hopes of Heaven

On the Palestinian West Bank during the 1990s, would-be suicide bombers felt hopeless, desperate, and very angry. Like many volunteers who join terrorist organizations, they believed they had to "do something." Many sacrificed their lives in hopes of winning a better future for Palestinians. The suicide bombers believe that their actions will win them a blissful reward in heaven — although many Muslim scholars say that this hope is based on mistaken religious ideas.

Ideology

During the 1980s and 1990s, in countries as far apart as Peru and Nepal, hundreds of police, government officials, doctors, and teachers were killed by Maoist terrorists. These men and women followed the teachings of the former Chinese communist leader Mao Zedong. Mao's writings urge workers to participate in a "permanent revolution," in which ordinary people overthrow the ruling class and gain control of all political and economic power. The terrorists followed the example of Mao, who believed that his ruthless actions justified his goal.

Intimidation

In the 1990s, Northern Ireland's two principal warring factions, the Nationalists (Irish republicans) and the Loyalists (pro-British), each contained armed gangs and terrorist organizations. These two groups often attacked members of their own communities who befriended people from "enemy" backgrounds or who worked to bring about peace. Both sides claimed that this was necessary for "security" reasons. Because groups like these act outside the law, many terrorists live in fear of being betrayed. Their threats of violence and brutal tactics force others to help them — or to keep quiet — "or else." Bloody feuds and revenge killings are common among these groups.

(Above) Fighting in Chechnya between guerrillas and Russian soldiers has been fierce, with atrocities committed by both sides.

Al-Qaeda

Terrorist attacks can occur anywhere in the world, but some of the worst terrorist attacks happen in the Middle East, where many dangerous and determined terrorist organizations are based. One of the infamous terrorist groups is "*al-Qaeda*" ("The Base"). Founded in 1989 by Saudi Arabian millionaire Osama bin Laden, al-Qaeda aims to unite all Muslims and establish a world Islamic government. Al-Qaeda recruits members from all over the world for its terrorist activities.

CRIMINAL *involvement*

Just like criminals, terrorists often use violence to get what they want. For example, in Colombia, South America, terrorists and criminals share a common enemy — the Colombian government. Criminals supply weapons and ammunition to terrorists. In return, terrorists help criminals operate illegal businesses, especially the profitable trade in illicit drugs such as cocaine.

"One man's terrorist is another man's freedom-fighter."

A well-known saying

OSAMA bin Laden

Osama bin Laden was born in Saudi Arabia to a wealthy family in 1957. During the 1980s — with support from the United States — bin Laden fought against the Soviet invaders in Afghanistan. After Soviet troops left Afghanistan, he returned to Saudi Arabia, where he campaigned against the Saudi government and against Western influence and foreigners until he was expelled in 1991. In 1996, bin Laden returned to Afghanistan, which was ruled by fundamentalist Muslim Taliban. Bin Laden used his wealth to recruit and train his followers for terrorist missions.

Osama bin Laden (right) claims that he began his terrorist activities because of two issues that outraged him more than any others: The presence of non-Muslim western foreigners in Saudi Arabia, the birthplace of the prophet Muhammad; and the West's refusal to allow the Palestinians to have an independent homeland.

Muslim anger

In 1947, the United Nations declared the partition of Palestine into two nations — a Jewish state (Israel) and an Arab state. When Israel became an independent nation in 1948, Arab nations in the region declared war on the new country. Israel won that war and absorbed most of what was to have been the new Arab state. Since that time, Israel has fought several wars with neighboring Arab states, and in 1967, it occupied the West Bank region (then part of Jordan) and the Gaza Strip (formerly occupied by Egypt), where many Palestinian Arabs lived. In 1987, Palestinians launched an unsuccessful *intifada* ("uprising") in an attempt to win back Arab land in the occupied territories. Arabs in many Middle Eastern lands and Muslims in other parts of the world offered their support.

Fundamentalism

After the creation of Israel and with the domination of Western culture, radical Muslim reformers began to attract more supporters. Their message called for a return to pure Islamic beliefs and for *shariyah* ("Muslim holy law"). Some supporters disliked Western secular (nonreligious) beliefs. Others were inspired by the 1979 Iranian Islamic Revolution to defend Muslim countries against perceived threats from Israel, the U.S., and the Soviet Union.

Muslim Jihad

In 1979, Soviet troops invaded Afghanistan. The Afghan *mujahedin* (Muslim guerrilla fighters) fought back ferociously, claiming that their struggle was a *jihad* (holy war). To help in the

JIHAD *against America*

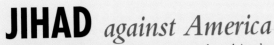

In 1998, al-Qaeda issued a statement. In it, members claimed to represent "the World Islamic Front for Jihad Against Jews and Crusaders." They declared that it was "the duty of all Muslims to kill U.S. citizens — civilians or military — and their allies everywhere." In Arabic, "*jihad*" means "holy war." It can also mean many other kinds of personal struggle, such as practicing self-discipline in everyday life, working hard, and adopting an honest, productive lifestyle.

An Afghan fighter is ready for action during the U.S. campaign against the Taliban in November 2001.

fight, Osama bin Laden sent Muslim volunteers — many of them extremists from different nation trained in terror tactics. This new terrorist group was the organization that became al-Qaeda. Ironically, the United States supported bin Laden's efforts against the Soviet Union in Afghanistan.

Muslim impact

Members of al-Qaeda soon became active in other parts of the world and attracted even more recruits. From the mid-1990s on, people thought to have ties with al-Qaeda have been linked to several attacks and terrorist plots, including: the shooting down of U.S. Army helicopters in Somalia, Africa; a 1993 attack on the World Trade Center in New York City that killed six people; plans to kill the Pope and President Bill Clinton in the Philippines; the bombing of U.S. embassies in Kenya and Tanzania; plans to kill U.S. and Israeli tourists in Jordan, and, in 2000, the attack on the *USS Cole* in Yemen. Then its members began planning the most ambitious attack yet — the September 11, 2001, hijackings. Most of the men who carried out this attack were chosen for their aviation knowledge. Several had studied aircraft construction in Germany during the 1990s. Others took flying lessons in Europe and in U.S. flying schools. All the attackers had entered the U.S. legally using valid visas.

SEPTEMBER 11, 2001

It was the height of the rush hour on a beautiful September morning in New York City. Thousands of men and women streamed into work, including staff from the many international businesses with offices in the World Trade Center (WTC). People around the world recognized the WTC's 110-story twin towers as proud symbols of free enterprise and capitalism. On a normal weekday, more than fifty thousand people worked in the towers.

FIRST HIJACK

At 8:00 A.M. Eastern Daylight Time (EDT), American Airlines Flight 11, a Boeing 767 jet bound for Los Angeles, took off from Logan Airport in Boston. At 8:28 A.M., four hijackers, led by Mohammad Atta (right) and armed with box cutters took over the cockpit. Air-traffic controllers on the ground overheard the hijackers say, "Don't do anything foolish. You are not going to get hurt. We have other planes."

FLIGHT 175

At about 8:30 A.M., passengers and crew on board a second aircraft, United Airlines Flight 175, were overpowered by five more hijackers. That flight left Boston for Los Angeles at 8:14 A.M. with sixty-five people on board. In their struggle to gain control of the plane, the hijackers stabbed one of the crew members. A brave female flight attendant notified air traffic controllers about the situation.

NORAD

At 8:40 A.M., the U.S. Federal Aviation Administration (FAA) sent an alert to NORAD (the North American Aerospace Defense Command), the military organization that guards the skies over the United States and Canada. Three minutes later, the FAA sent another alert warning of a second suspected hijacking. NORAD "scrambled" (urgently launched) two F-15 jet fighters from Otis Air National Guard Base in Falmouth, Massachusetts, to intercept the hijacked planes.

DISASTER STRIKES

Instead of heading west from Boston toward its scheduled destination, American Airlines Flight 11 flew south toward New York City The plane's speed increased to about 500 miles per hour (800 kilometers per hour). It crashed into the north tower of the World Trade Center between the 95th and 103rd floors. The impact killed all 92 passengers, crew, and four hijackers on board and hundreds of people in the north tower. Anyone above the impact site was trapped in the building, including about eighty chefs, waiters, and kitchen staff who worked at the Windows on the World restaurant on the 106th floor. Meanwhile, viewers in the U.S. and all over the world watched in horror and disbelief as live television reports showed black smoke billowing from the north tower of the World Trade Center.

VIEWPOINT

"At 8:48, as I was sitting in my chair, I felt a tremendous jolt. My office chair rolled in one direction and then the opposite direction. During the sway, I could hear the grinding of concrete and steel. Burning metal pieces and tons of paper were flying outside the south windows and falling to the ground below.

Several people just stared out the windows, completely shocked at what they were seeing. I really thought the building was going to fall down right then and there."

— World Trade Center employee

DISASTER AT THE SOUTH TOWER

As they looked through their viewfinders, camera news crews were appalled to see a second aircraft — United Flight 175 — heading for the World Trade Center. At 9:03 A.M., millions of stunned TV viewers and workers in nearby buildings watched as Flight 175 crashed into the south tower. The plane hit the building at about the eightieth floor, forcing a massive cloud of dust, smoke, and vaporized aircraft fuel out the other side of the tower.

THE PRESIDENT IS TOLD   09:10

Most people thought the first plane hit the World Trade Center in a tragic accident. As television news cameras captured the approach and impact of the second plane, however, onlookers and U.S. government officials immediately feared an attack. President Bush received the news at 9:10 A.M. while he was reading to students at a Sarasota, Florida, grade school. Within ten minutes, the Federal Bureau of Investigation (FBI) began investigating the incident as a possible terrorist attack.

FIRST FIREFIGHTERS

By 9:29 A.M., the first police officers, firefighters, and ambulance crews arrived at the World Trade Center. As the rescue teams started walking up, office workers from below the plane-crash levels of both towers began leaving the building. Meanwhile, in Florida, a grim-faced President Bush told reporters, "We have had a national tragedy."

VIEWPOINT

"We saw both towers on fire. Both towers had similar, charred, massive holes in their sides, and bright red flames were coming out of the damaged areas. It was unbelievable.

By this time, my colleagues were crying and looking at the towers in disbelief. They had their arms around one another. We walked to the corner of Fulton and Broadway, and I saw something horrible. I recognized a piece of a jet airliner's front landing gear.

It was on the street, underneath what looked like a large pool of blood. There was so much blood on the street."

— a World Trade Center worker, who escaped from the building

A New York firefighter, blackened by the smoke and dust of the burning buildings, helps people to safety.

HEART OF THE GOVERNMENT

At 9:40 A.M., about an hour and twenty minutes after takeoff, a third aircraft — American Airlines Flight 77 bound from Washington, D.C. to Los Angeles — crashed into the Pentagon in Arlington, Virgina, just outside Washington, D.C. One of the most secure buildings in the world, the fortress-like Pentagon is the command center for the U.S. Department of Defense. Flight 77 exploded in a massive fireball that collapsed five floors of the Pentagon. The impact killed all 64 people, including the five hijackers, on board Flight 77. About 190 Pentagon staff members also died.

WASHINGTON IN DANGER

By 9:45 A.M., security experts feared that the president's life and the lives of his staff were in danger. Key buildings in Washington, D.C., including the White House (home and headquarters of the U.S. president) and the Capitol (which houses government offices) were evacuated. The government also stopped all scheduled commercial flights from leaving U.S. airports and ordered planes already in the air to land as soon as possible. The last time all U.S. air traffic shut down was in the early 1960s for testing of the Sky Shield air defenses.

THE FOURTH PLANE

`10:06`

At 10:06 A.M. United Airlines Flight 93 heading to San Francisco from Newark, New Jersey, crashed in a field near Shanksville, Pennsylvania. All forty-five passengers, including four hijackers armed with knives and a box they claimed was a bomb, were killed. Investigators learned from cell phone accounts that Flight 93's passengers overpowered the hijackers just before the crash. Authorites believe that the aircraft's intended target was an important government building in Washington, D.C., such as the White House or Capitol.

VIEWPOINT

"I want to reassure the American people that the full resources of the federal government are working to assist local authorities to save lives and help the victims of these attacks... The resolve of our great nation is being tested. But make no mistake: we will show the world that we will pass this test."

— President G. W. Bush, September 11, 2001

COLLAPSE

`10:05`

In New York, scenes of unimaginable horror unfolded. Workers on the lower floors of the north and south towers of the World Trade Center struggled to find their way down steps through blinding clouds of poisonous smoke. Some people lost their way in the dark and became trapped. Others perished, gasping and choking, as heat and fumes scorched their lungs. Higher up in the towers, above the impact zone, men and women jumped to their deaths from office windows. Then suddenly, with an appalling rumble, the south tower collapsed. Like many modern office buildings, the World Trade Center had been built around a framework of steel. But the aircraft crash carried about 10,000 gallons (38,000 liters) of flammable aircraft fuel that soaked the building. As this fuel blazed, temperatures around the impact zone soared to more than 1,450 degrees Farenheit (800 degrees Centigrade). The steel frame softened and buckled, causing the concrete floors and walls it once supported to collapse. Hundreds of office workers — together with the police, firefighters, and ambulance crews who were helping them leave the building — were crushed under hundreds of thousands of tons of rubble as the south tower crumbled.

SEPTEMBER 11, 2001

THE NORTH TOWER CRUMBLES

The deadly roar of the south tower collapsing had hardly died away when the north tower also crumpled and crashed to the ground. People outside the World Trade Center ran for their lives as a massive cloud of dust and smoke swirled around the ruins and shards of glass and slabs of concrete rained down on them from above. Hundreds more World Trade Center workers and emergency personnel were killed. In less than two hours, one of the most visible symbols of American free trade had been destroyed.

PROTECTING THE PRESIDENT

For safety reasons, President Bush was flown to the isolated Offutt Air Force Base in rural Nebraska at 1:20 P.M. Minutes later, U.S. army and navy commanders sent seven warships to guard the east coast of the U.S. Extra fighter planes also patrolled the skies above Washington, D.C. and New York City. At 1:50 P.M., the mayor of Washington, D.C. declared a state of emergency in the capital, giving police and soldiers sweeping powers to act against suspected terrorists.

14:48

Although police officers, firefighters, and ambulance crew lost many of their colleagues, they began searching through the rubble of the collapsed World Trade Center. It soon became clear that very few people in or near either tower survived the collapse. Searchers found just five survivors in the first twenty-four hours. Long before then, New Yorkers were beginning to realize the scale of the tragedy that had hit them. In an emotional statement, four hours after the first tower collapsed, New York City's mayor, Rudolph Giuliani, declared that the death toll might be "more than any of us can bear."

20:30

At 8:30 P.M. on September 11, 2001, President Bush made an official TV broadcast to the nation. In it, he spoke of the deep shock at the attack, but how the citizens of the United States would stand together and beat the terrorists.

BROADCAST *to the nation*

"Today, our fellow citizens, our way of life, our very freedom came under attack in a series of deliberate and deadly terrorist acts. These acts of mass murder were intended to frighten our nation into chaos and retreat. But they have failed. Terrorist attacks can shake the foundations of our biggest buildings, but they cannot touch the foundation of America."

— President Bush addressed the nation

As the smoke and dust slowly settled over the crumpled remains of the World Trade Center, the citizens of New York City were left with a gash in their famous skyline and a hole in their hearts. The devastated site soon became known as "Ground Zero." President Bush summed up their thoughts: "None of us will ever forget this day."

For weeks after the event, heartbreaking pleas for help, such as the one pictured below, were posted around Ground Zero by people hoping that their loved ones had somehow survived the calamity.

We Need Your Help

Giovanna "Gennie" Gambale

27 years old 5'6"
Brown hair, brown eyes
Last seen on 102nd fl of World Trade Center 1
(E-Speed/Cantor-Fitzgerald)
Call with any information 718-624-0465

A terrible toll

In the days following the terrorist attacks, emergency workers continued to search through the rubble at the different sites, but they found very few survivors. The final death toll from the terrorist attacks rose to more than three thousand. Many thousands more men, women, and children mourned loved ones, colleagues, and neighbors killed in the tragedy.

In ruins

New Yorkers also suffered whenever they saw the ruined buildings at Ground Zero. As engineers and construction workers labored to clear rubble and make the site safe, one volunteer rescuer said in disbelief, "I never thought I'd see the World Trade Center pass me by in a dump truck." Some experts feared that shock waves from the collapsing towers may have destabilized the surrounding ground, and that the Hudson River might flood the whole business district of New York. Fortunately, their predictions did not come true, but many buildings close to Ground Zero proved to be seriously damaged, and one collapsed.

America's finest

There was just a little good news among the reports of death and destruction. As the survivors recalled

CASUALTY *statistics*

World Trade Center deaths	2,792	Deaths on aircraft	265
World Trade Center injured	2,261	Firefighter deaths	343
Pentagon deaths	125	Law-enforcement officer deaths	75

and heroism by members of the emergency services, especially the firefighters. They remembered how rescue teams courageously entered the burning towers to lead office workers to safety, even though firefighters knew the buildings were likely to collapse. Ambulance crews, too, had rushed towards the inferno as others were running away in fear of their lives. These brave people were hailed as "America's finest." Mayor Giuliani was also praised for his inspiring leadership and many world leaders sent messages of sympathy and support.

CONDEMNATION *of the attacks*

"Yesterday was indeed a dark day in our history, an appalling offence against peace, a terrible assault against human dignity."
— Pope John Paul II

"This is a war between good and evil and between humanity and the bloodthirsty..."
— Ariel Sharon, prime minister of Israel

"We were completely shocked... It's unbelievable, unbelievable, unbelievable..."
— Yasir Arafat, president of the Palestinian Authority

"I condemn them utterly..."
— Kofi Annan, Secretary General of the United Nations

A blow to business

The terrorists' choice of the World Trade Center as their target was deliberate. They hoped that confidence in U.S. business would collapse, along with the towers. This did not happen, but for the first time in more than fifty years, people started to question the economic power of the United States. Before the attack, the financial stability of the U.S. seemed unshakeable. Afterward, many customers and investors became very cautious, people cut back on air travel, and the U.S. economy slowed down.

President George W. Bush addresses members of the emergency services near the Ground Zero.

CLIMATE OF FEAR

Although most practicing Muslims were outraged by the terrorist attacks, many were treated with deep suspicion afterwards.

Changing climate

Before the attacks, Americans prided themselves on their free and easy ways. These ranged from welcoming strangers with few questions to the right to own a gun. The American way of life seemed safe and secure behind the nation's natural frontiers of deserts, mountains and oceans. Its armed forces were the strongest in the world.

What went wrong?

After the attacks, however, the United States no longer seemed like such a safe place to live. Once the shock of the terrorist attacks passed, people began asking questions — in particular, why had there been no warning? The two main intelligence organizations, the CIA (Central Intelligence Agency) and the FBI (Federal Bureau of Investigation), were accused of failing to recognize the clues that their intelligence agents had gathered. To prevent similar failures in the future, all U.S. security personnel throughout the world went on high alert. President Bush vowed to find those responsible for the September 11 attacks and to bring them to justice, promising an international "crusade [to] rid the world of evil-doers."

Homeland security

The U.S. government also set up a new department, responsible for homeland security. Controversially, police arrested hundreds of young (mostly Muslim) men and accused them of entering the U.S. illegally — even though most of the September 11 hijackers had entered the country legally. Airport travel within the United States and abroad became much more difficult, because all passengers now had to pass through much tighter security checks. Even seemingly innocent items, such as nail clippers and knitting needles, were banned from carry-on luggage. Delays caused by these travel checks and the fear of further terrorist attacks caused a sharp drop in the number of tourists visiting the U.S. Many Americans also cancelled their plans to travel abroad, whether on vacation or for business.

Deadly packages

In autumn 2001, this climate of fear worsened after packets of a mysterious white powder were mailed to government and news service offices in several U.S. cities. The packets contained spores ("seeds") of the deadly anthrax bacterium. Panic spread across the country, and hospitals stockpiled large amounts of antibiotics to use as antidotes. Officials believe the anthrax packets were probably mailed by a lone criminal, but no one knows for sure.

Biological warfare?

Intelligence experts warned that al-Qaeda or the governments that supported similar terrorist groups might launch a biological warfare

Throughout the anthrax crisis, U.S. Customs remained on heightened alert for any suspect material entering the country.

THE PRESIDENT'S *response*

"We are a different country than we were on September 10, sadder and less innocent, stronger and more united. And in the face of ongoing threats, determined and courageous. Our nation faces a threat to our freedoms, and the stakes could not be higher. We are the target of enemies who boast that they want to kill, kill all Americans, kill all Jews and kill all Christians…"

— President Bush, speaking two months after the attacks

attack against the United States. These fears deepened after the broadcast of a videotape of Osama bin Laden making fresh threats against the United States and its people. The smallpox virus was one of the "weapons" that could be used in such an attack. Even though smallpox was considered a "conquered" disease, the U.S. government decided to stock up on its supplies of smallpox vaccine, and many members of the military received smallpox vaccinations as a precaution.

"The terrorists seem to have succeeded much beyond their own expectations… I can't think of anything that has disrupted government so much since the Civil War."

James Thurber, a professor of American government, in reference to the U.S. postal service during the October–November 2001 anthrax scare

Two days after the tragedy, U.S. Secretary of State Colin Powell accused Osama bin Laden of being the mastermind behind the terrorist attacks. The U.S. government believed that al-Qaeda was the only group with enought money and resources to plan and execute such an attack. The world's attention focused on Afghanistan, where intelligence experts believed Osama bin Laden was hiding.

Many Taliban recruits (below) were uprooted young men from refugee camps on the border between Pakistan and Afghanistan. Poor and angry, they found the Taliban's radical version of Islam appealing.

The Taliban

Since 1989, when Soviet troops left Afghanistan, there had been no strong, settled government. Instead, the country was controlled by rival warlords. In 1996, a group of young Islamic militants, calling themselves the "*Taliban*" ("God's Students") seized control of most of Afghanistan, forcing government ministers to flee. Founded in 1994 by Afghan Muslim religious teacher Mullah Mohammad Omar, the Taliban at first fought lawlessness and corruption. The group attracted many recruits among poor, unemployed young men from villages in Afghanistan and from the large refugee camps across the border in Pakistan — where many Afghan families had lived in crowded, miserable conditions since the Soviet Union invaded their country in 1979. Taliban recruits were appalled by the civil wars that were ruining their country. They also hated the growing popularity of Western entertainment, fashions, and secular, scientific ideas among wealthy Afghan people .

A CONTINUING *problem*

It was relatively easy for the U.S. military to overthrow the Taliban in Afghanistan, but establishing a satisfactory peace has proved more difficult. Despite help from the ISAF (the International Security Assistance Force), fighting among rival warlords continues. Afghan people are still desperately poor, and severe droughts worsened their situation. The new government only controls Kabul, Afghaistan's capital. Finally, the financial support and expert assistance promised by the international community for the rebuilding efforts have been tragically slow to reach the people who need it.

Strict Islam

By 1999, Taliban forces numbered about thirty thousand militia (volunteer soldiers). They also had tanks and aircraft

(left) U.S. troops set off for Kabul, the capital of Afghanistan.
(below) British troops blow up enemy missiles in Afghanistan.

captured from Afghan warlords. Troops of the Taliban patrolled Afghan villages and towns, forcing their own strict view of Islam on all citizens. They closed schools, banned music and dancing, and forbade all women (even doctors and nurses) from working outside the home. Hoping to spread their own fundamentalist views, they supported Muslim terrorist groups in other countries, including al-Qaeda.

Ready for war

On September 14, 2001, the U.S. government mobilized fifty thousand reserve troops and sent aircraft and warships to bases within easy reach of Afghanistan. President Bush called for the Taliban to hand over Osama bin Laden "dead or alive." The Taliban refused. Instead, they asked Muslims all over the world to begin a "holy war" against the United States.

Attack and surrender

On October 7, 2001, U.S. forces attacked Afghanistan with bombs and heavy artillery. Faced with this massive firepower, the Taliban had no chance. Its members were killed or went into hiding. By December, a new civilian government, backed by the U.S. and most of the international community, began the daunting task of reuniting and rebuilding poverty-stricken, war-torn Afghanistan.

> "By destroying camps and disrupting communications, we'll make it more difficult for the terror network to train new recruits and coordinate their evil plans. Initially, the terrorists may burrow deeper into caves and other... hiding places. Our military action is also designed to clear the way for sustained, comprehensive and relentless operations to drive them out and bring them to justice."
>
> **President Bush gives his reasons for invading Afghanistan**

New allies, new enemies

The September 11 attacks meant that the United States had new enemies as well as new friends. When news of the terrorist attacks spread around the world, government leaders hurried to express their shock and horror, and to offer the U.S. their support. Even nations traditionally hostile to the U.S., such as Libya and Iran, sent messages of sympathy. President Jacques Chirac of France (a frequent critic of U.S. policy) declared, "We are all Americans."

Strong support

In return for these friendly words and promises of cooperation, the United States offered strong support to countries fighting terrorism on their own soil, including Russia, China, and Israel. U.S. government officials stopped criticizing harsh anti-terrorist actions, such as the use of a deadly knock-out gas to stun terrorists holding hostages in a theater in Moscow, Russia. Before September 11, they might have protested that these acts broke international agreements on human rights. On a visit to Russia, President Bush declared,

President George W. Bush thanks Russian Federation President Vladimir Putin for his support in the war on terror. Putin's help signaled the beginning of an improved relationship between the U.S. and Russia.

"When I was in high school, Russia was an enemy. Now high school students can know that Russia is a friend."

Worldwide war

President Bush described his troops' invasion of Afghanistan as a new kind of conflict: a war on many fronts, against terrorists who operate in more than sixty different countries.

Suspicions

U.S. diplomats warned all nations, including allies such as Saudi Arabia, not to tolerate Islamic extremists. U.S. army commanders made precautionary plans to invade unstable countries like Somalia, Africa, where they believed that al-Qaeda terrorists were hiding and planning further attacks. The U.S. government also put pressure on the Palestinians to replace their leader, Yasir Arafat, because they believed he was not sufficiently "tough against terrorists," and they alleged that Syria "might be" sponsoring terror. The U.S. also kept a close watch on Pakistan, after Muslim terrorists there killed U.S. embassy staff members who were attending church. They also killed Daniel Pearl, a respected U.S. journalist, because he was an American and a Jew.

Contrasting views

The U.S. call for a worldwide war against terror provoked contrasting reactions in many other countries. In Britain, the strongly pro-American government passed new laws giving police the right to imprison terrorist suspects before they had committed any crimes. Governments in Indonesia and the Philippines also cracked down on terrorist groups related to al-Queda. Many nations protested, however, when the U.S. government imprisoned hundreds of suspected

SUPPORT *from friends*

"The entire international community should unite in the struggle against terrorism."
—Vladimir Putin, president of Russia

"We, the democracies of the world, are going to have to come together to fight and eradicate this evil completely from our world."

— Tony Blair, prime minister of Britain

"An attack on one is an attack on all..."

— Lord Robertson, Secretary General of NATO
(North Atlantic Treaty Organization)

Cuban leader Fidel Castro (above) was highly critical of the reaction by U.S. leaders to the September 11 attacks.

SYMPATHY *from enemies*

"Irrespective of the conflict with America, it is a human duty to show sympathy with the American people, and be one with them at these horrifying and awesome events which are bound to awaken human conscience."

— Muammar al-Qaddafi, Libyan leader

"[We offer] deep regret and sympathy... It is an international duty to try and undermine terrorism."

— Mohammad Khatam, president of Iran

terrorists from Afghanistan at the U.S. military base in Guantanamo Bay, Cuba. Fidel Castro, Cuba's communist leader and a long-time enemy of the United States, said that the U.S. reaction to the events of September 11 was "worse than the original attacks." As U.S. foreign policy became increasingly tougher, other countries wondered whether the United States was squandering the sympathy it had received on September 11, 2001.

"Axis of evil"

In January 2002, President Bush claimed that North Korea, Iraq, and Iran supported terrorism and formed an "axis of evil." Bush promised that the U.S. would hunt down any terrorists — especially in those countries.

A monument in North Korea depicts the communist struggle (below). The country is on the U.S's "axis of evil" list of hostile countries.

"What America is tasting now is something insignificant compared to what we have tasted for scores of years. Our nation (the Islamic world) has been tasting this humiliation and this degradation for more than 80 years. Its sons are killed, its blood is shed, its sanctuaries are attacked and no-one hears and no-one heeds."

Osama bin Laden justifies his terrorist attacks

THE WAR ON TERROR

President Bush met with British Prime Minister Tony Blair prior to the second Gulf War.

A United Nations' team of inspectors searched Iraq for weapons of mass destruction before the U.S. and coalition forces invaded in March, 2003.

Weapons of mass destruction

For more than a year after the September 11 terrorist attacks, the U.S. government issued further warnings. It declared that any nation found to have weapons of mass destruction (WMD) would be considered a threat to future world peace and a legitimate (lawful) target for attack. The United States singled out Iraq — a former ally — as a special danger. In 1990, Iraqi dictator Saddam Hussein sparked the first Gulf War when it invaded neighboring Kuwait in an attempt to control its vast oil reserves. A broad U.S.-led international coalition defeated Hussein's forces within months, but did not oust him from power. Hussein remained an enemy of the West, and after September 11, the United States began accusing him of supporting Palestinian terrorists and building biological weapons loaded with germs and poisonous gas.

The United States acts

Although Saddam Hussein was hated and feared by his own people and had very few allies abroad, many nations that supported the U.S.'s "worldwide war against terrorism" were uneasy about the U.S. threat to attack Iraq. Members of the United Nations wanted to wait until inspectors discovered clear evidence that Iraq harbored weapons of mass destruction. Despite the lack of agreement with United Nations' policy, the U.S., its close ally, Britain, and some smaller nations followed through with the plan. In spring 2003, coalition forces invaded Iraq and ousted Saddam Hussein.

Reasons for war

Since September 11, 2001, the United States and its allies have claimed that the war on terrorism is justified. They believe that their massive military strength will one day defeat al-Qaeda, or at least stop any government or nation that offers support to terrorists. Critics view these anti-terrorist actions in differently. They claim that U.S.-led wars, especially in Iraq, are thinly disguised attempts to impose Western secular (non-religious) values on other countries, especially Muslim ones, and to take control of the world's most valuable energy resource — oil.

Tough tactics, human rights

The United States's determination to fight terrorism with tough tactics made many citizens feel proud of their nation's strength. Other U.S. citizens and legislators felt the government's actions raised a troublesome question: Despite the worldwide threat of terrorism, could the U.S. government justify all of its anti-terrorist measures — or were human rights now just a luxury that no twenty-first-century nation could afford to uphold? Critics of the United States also argue that, in the hunt for terrorist suspects since September 11, 2001, the U.S.and its allies ignored some of their most cherished legal principles — especially the right of suspects to be believed innocent until proved guilty.

The smoke and flames of war form an ominous backdrop for this massive statue of Saddam Hussein. After a campaign of precision bombing, U.S. and British forces held most of Iraq within a month.

BIN LADEN *speaks*

"... senior officials have spoken in America, starting with the head of infidels worldwide, Bush. They have come out in force with their men, and have turned even the countries that belong to Islam with this treachery, and they want to wag their tail at God, to fight Islam, to suppress people in the name of terrorism..."

Osama bin Laden claims that the United States intends to use its war against terrorism as an excuse to control Muslim lands.

The September 11 disaster is still fresh in the minds of most Americans. Every year, many honor victims of the tragedy. These Tennessee firefighters commemorate other firefighters who lost their lives while working to save others.

On May 5, 2003, President Bush claimed that "al-Qaeda is on the run." Unfortunately, before the end of that month, terrorists believed to be linked to al-Qaeda staged two attacks that killed and injured hundreds in Saudi Arabia and Morocco. Terrorist scares in East Africa and Southeast Asia, plus hints of new attacks in the U.S., suggested that the threat of terror continued.

A waiting game

Experts believe that most of these terrorist attacks were the work of al-Qaeda "sleepers" — people who had been recruited long before September 11, 2001. They had been ordered to stay hidden, and lead unremarkable lives until they were ordered to act. Intelligence experts also acknowledged that there were probably thousands of trained al-Qaeda supporters

The United States declared any suspected terrorist, such as the man dressed in orange below, an "unlawful combatant" — a unique status that denies a person the rights guaranteed an ordinary prisoner of war.

WORLD *view*

Has the world changed since September 11, 2001?

YES: *"My world has changed a great deal. I have become more proud of my country, even if the world seems to look at my country in a negative light."*
April Liesel, Los Angeles County, California — September 11, 2002

NO: *"There has not been any change in the political philosophy, social set-up, business system, means of production, educational system, or views on human rights. No one is born a terrorist. It is resentment and helplessness that drives a man to resort to this action."*
Professor Mukhtar Ali Naqvi, Orlando, Florida — September 11, 2002

ready and waiting to commit fresh terrorist outrages in almost forty countries. Although the United States and its allies could easily win conventional wars in Iraq and Afghanistan, they could not as easily defeat the largest and best-organized terrorist organization the world had ever seen.

A "fact of life?"

People began to ask, "What should the world do next?" How should governments deal with terrorism? Did police, politicians, soldiers, and citizens simply have to accept that terrorism was now "a fact of life," like the weather? Or should they fight against it? If so, should they hunt down terrorists and terrorist suspects in any manner possible — even in at the risk of compromising democratic principles? Or should nations that promote freedom and democracy continue to uphold justice, liberty, and human rights?

Still in shock

In many ways, the international community has yet to recover from the shock of the September 11 terrorist attacks. Many people are still deeply saddened and horrified by the tragedy. Events since the U.S. terrorist attacks suggest that massive military firepower

Do peace talks stand a chance? In June 2003, a poster in Jerusalem urges Jews to reject President Bush's "road map." Bush's plan aims to reach a peace settlement between Israel and the Palestinians and includes the establishment of an independent Palestinian state.

alone may not stop the violence. People continue to seek other ways to bring peace to nations through political negotiations and economic reforms.

Time will tell

People looking for alternative solutions to the threat of terrorism understand that simply removing the factors that make people decide to become terrorists will not solve the worldwide terror problem overnight. Sadly, there will always be activists with extreme religious or political views who will never agree to change. Hope instead lies with those people dedicated to ending injustice and working for equality — which offers the best chance of a brighter future for everyone. The far-reaching aftermath of the September 11 terrorist attacks created new opportunities to ponder these many issues.

THE WAY *forward*

"It is a sad confirmation that despite the rhetoric [fine words] and technological advances of modern human beings, violence is still the preferred method of dealing with problems. More violence will not solve the problem and power should not be measured in terms of military strength. The only way that September 11 could possibly change the world is if it caused us to wake up to the fact that we all share this planet and that peace is NOT achieved through war."
Beth Strachan, Vancouver, Canada — September 11, 2002

1200 B.C.–1896

- circa 1200 B.C.: Jewish prophet Moses leads the Israelites to Canaan, the "Promised Land" (present-day Israel), given to them by God.

- circa A.D. 570–632: Lifetime of the Prophet Muhammad, an Arabian religious teacher. Muslims believe Muhammad was God's greatest messenger, and the last.

- 1098–1197: Christian soldiers (Crusaders) occupy the Holy Land.

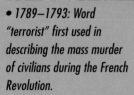

- 1789–1793: Word "terrorist" first used in describing the mass murder of civilians during the French Revolution.

- 1880–1953: Lifetime of Abd al-Aziz Ibn Saud, who campaigned for independence for Arabia and supported the strict Wahhabi movement for Islamic religious reform.

1897–1946

- 1897: First Zionist Congress calls for a separate independent Jewish homeland.

- 1917: British Foreign Secretary issues statement (the "Balfour Declaration") supporting an independent Jewish state.

- 1932: Saudi Arabia becomes an independent state. It grows rich after oil is discovered there in 1938.

- 1941: American President Franklin D. Roosevelt makes his "Four Freedoms" speech proclaiming human rights (freedom of worship, speech, expression, and from want and fear)

1947–1978

- 1947: United Nations divides Palestine into Jewish and Arab states.

- 1948: Israel becomes independent.

- 1967: Israel occupies the West Bank, where many Palestinians live.

- 1970s: Palestinian terrorists hijack three aircraft in Jordan (1970) and kill members of the Israeli Olympic Team in Munich, Germany (1972).

- 1976: The Hamas Islamic Resistance Movement is founded by Sheik Ahmad Yassin. Originally nonmilitant, it began using increasingly violent means during the 1990s, including the tactic of suicide bombing.

1979–1986

- 1979: Soviet troops invade Afghanistan. Afghan mujahedin (Muslim guerrilla fighters) declare a holy war against them.

- 1979: Muslim fundamentalists overthrow the Shah (king) in Iran. Radical Islamic leader Ayatollah Khomeini returns from exile to lead the Islamic Revolution.

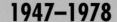

1987–1993

- **1987:** An intifada (uprising) is launched by Palestinians in protest against Israeli occupation of the West Bank and the Gaza Strip. They kill many Israeli civilians in suicide bombing attacks. Israelis retaliate by demolishing buildings where Palestinian terrorists are suspected of hiding.

- **1989:** Saudi Arabian millionaire Osama bin Laden founds al-Qaeda ("the Base") to unite all Muslims and set up a world Islamic government.

- **1993:** Muslim terrorists, suspected of links with al-Qaeda, attack U.S. Army helicopters in Somalia.

- **1993:** a bomb kills six in New York City's World Trade Center Twin Towers; al-Qaeda terrorists suspected.

1994–2000

- **1994:** Afghan Muslim religious teacher Mullah Mohammad Omar founds the Taliban ("God's Students") religious movement in Afghanistan.

- **1995:** al-Qaeda plots to kill U.S. President Bill Clinton in the Philippines.

- **1996:** Taliban take control of Afghanistan, and introduce strict Muslim laws throughout the country.

- **1996:** Osama bin Laden is expelled from Saudi Arabia and moves to Taliban-controlled Afghanistan.

- **1998:** al-Qaeda declares that it is the duty of all Muslims to kill U.S. citizens and their allies.

- **1998:** al-Qaeda blows up the U.S. embassies in Kenya and Tanzania, killing many people.

- **2000:** Muslim terrorists linked to al-Qaeda attack the USS Cole, while it is in harbor in the Middle Eastern country of Yemen.

2001–2002

- **September 11, 2001:** Al-Qaeda terrorists hijack four U.S. aircraft. Two fly into and collapse the twin towers of the World Trade Center in New York City; one crashes into the Pentagon in Washington, D.C., and the other crashes in a Pennsylvania field.

- **September–October 2001:** President Bush promises to bring terrorists to justice. The United States receives support from many world leaders, including its former enemy, Russia. Department of Homeland Security set up in the U.S. New security checks on air passengers. Mysterious anthrax attacks spread panic across the eastern United States.

- **October 2001:** U.S. forces lead an attack on Afghanistan. The Taliban disperse.

- **January 2002:** President Bush makes speech labeling North Korea, Iraq, and Iran an "axis of evil."

2002–2003

- **October 2002:** Muslim terrorists fighting for independence from Russia in Chechnya hold hostages in a theater in Moscow, Russia.

- **October 2002:** Muslim terrorists linked to al-Qaeda attack nightclubs in Bali, Indonesia, causing many deaths.

- **March 2003:** The U.S. and its allies, including Britain, Australia, and Poland, invade Iraq.

- **May 2003:** President Bush claims that "al-Qaeda is on the run." Days later, al-Qaeda terrorists attack civilians in Saudi Arabia and Morocco.

al-Qaeda ("the Base") a terrorist organization founded by Osama bin Laden in 1989 with the aim of uniting all Muslims and establishing a world Islamic government. Al-Qaeda's two main grievances are the presence of "infidels" in Arabia, the birthplace of the prophet Muhammad, and the failure of the West to offer the Palestinians an independent state.

anthrax a bacterial disease that can be transmitted to humans from sheep and cattle. Anthrax may be manufactured as a biological weapon and can kill if inhaled.

"axis of evil" a term used by President George W. Bush to describe the countries deemed actively hostile to U.S. interests, namely North Korea, Iraq, and Iran.

biological weapons toxins, bacteria, or viruses manufactured for use in warfare.

Chechnya a region in the southwest Russian Federation where ethnic Chechens are fighting for independence from the government based in Moscow.

CIA (Central Intelligence Agency) the United States's intelligence-gathering organization that operates around the world.

crusade a Christian military expedition with the aim of recovering control of the Holy Land from the Muslims; the term is also used to describe a strong campaign in favor of a moral cause.

dictatorship a state in which all power rests in the hands of one individual, the dictator.

ETA a terrorist movement for independence for the Basque region in the Pyrenees Mountains of northern Spain and southwest France.

F-15 the fighter jet aircraft scrambled on September 11, 2001 to patrol the skies over the northeastern U.S. after the terrorist attacks.

FBI (Federal Bureau of Investigation) the United States's nationwide law-enforcement organization.

fundamentalism the strict observance of the ancient or traditional beliefs of a religion.

guerrilla a member of an independent rebel group who uses unconventional, violent tactics to fight for a particular cause.

Hamas a Palestinian resistance movement founded by Sheik Yassin Ahmad in 1976. It is notable for its use of violence, particularly suicide bombing.

hijack to seize control of a means of transportation and force it to a different destination.

Holy Land a region of the Middle East divided between Syria, Israel, Jordan, and the disputed Palestinian territory that is sacred to three of the world's great faiths: Christianity, Judaism, and Islam.

Homeland Security a federal government department established by President George W. Bush after September 11, 2001 to improve internal security within the United States.

infidel a derogatory term used by Muslim fundamentalists to describe any non-Muslim.

IRA (Irish Republican Army) a terrorist organization founded in 1919 to unite Northern Ireland (part of the United Kingdom) with the Republic of Ireland in the south.

Islam the religion of Muslims.

jihad Arabic for "holy war."

Middle East the region along the southern and eastern shores of the Mediterranean Sea from Morocco to Pakistan and from Turkey south, including the entire Arabian Peninsula and the Persian Gulf.

Molotov cocktail a crude bomb made of flammable liquid in a bottle with a rag wick that is lit and thrown at a target to explode and burn.

Maoists followers of the teachings of Chinese communist leader Mao Zedong (1893–1976).

mujahedin Muslim guerrilla fighters.

NATO (North Atlantic Treaty Organization) a group of Western nations that formed in 1949 to protect each other in the event of an attack, especially from the apparent threat posed by communist countries in eastern Europe.

NORAD (North American Aerospace Defense Command) a military organization that guards the North American skies over the United States and Canada.

Ottoman Empire a Muslim empire concentrated in the Middle East with headquarters in present-day Turkey that existed from the fourteen century until 1922. Its influence spread throughout the Persian Gulf region to northern Africa and Eastern Europe, and its navy controlled the eastern portion of the Mediterranean Sea.

pre-emptive strike a term for using a military action or occupation to prevent the development of an even more dire or undesired set of circumstances.

Promised Land in the Jewish faith, the land promised to the Jews by God — "the land of Canaan" between the Jordan River and the Mediterranean Sea (present-day Israel).

"road map" the name for the U.S.-sponsored Israeli-Palestinian peace initiative of 2003, by which a series of dates and steps toward peace is to be agreed upon by both sides with the eventual aim of peace and an independent Palestinian state.

secular nonreligious.

shariyah Muslim holy law based on the teachings of the Muslim holy book, the Koran (*al-Qur'an* in Arabic).

Shining Path the group of Maoist guerrillas in Peru.

Soviet Union (Union of Soviet Socialist Republics; the USSR) a country formed after the Russian Revolution of October 1917. The Soviet Union dissolved in 1991.

suicide bomber a terrorist who deliberately kills himself or herself in the act of detonating a bomb.

Taliban ("God's students") the fundamentalist Muslim movement founded in Afghanistan in 1994 by Mullah Mohammad Omar that introduced a very strict Islamic regime and banned music and any form of occupation for women outside the home.

Tamil Tigers Sri Lankan terrorist guerrillas whose aim is to establish an independent homeland for the ethnic Tamil minority in northern Sri Lanka, free from control by the majority Sinhalese. Throughout the 1970s and 1980s, the Tamil Tigers ran camps that trained terrorists and carried out many suicide bombing attacks.

terrorism the use of violence or intimidation for political ends.

United Nations (UN) an international organization based in New York City that promotes human dignity and peace among nations.

Wahhabism a strict Islamic religious reform movement that hopes to purify Islam.

weapons inspectors experts that search for certain types of weapons in countries not permitted by the UN to keep such weapons.

Weapons of Mass Destruction (WMD) biological, chemical, or nuclear devices that can kill a large number of people at once within a specific location or within a very short time period.

FURTHER INFORMATION

Books

Al-Qaeda: Osama bin Laden's Army of Terrorists. Inside the World's Most Infamous Terrorist Organization. Phillip Marquiles (Rosen)

Keeping the Peace: The U.S. Military Responds to Terror. Spirit of America, a Nation Responds to the Events of 11 September 2001. Richard Mintzer (Chelsea House)

The History of Terrorism. Terrorism Library (series). Robert Taylor (Lucent)

Jerusalem or Death: Palestinian Terrorism. Terrorist Dossier. Samuel Katz (Lerner)

The Terrorist Attacks of September 11, 2001. Landmark Events in American History (series). Dale Anderson (World Almanac Library)

Terrorism in America. Tricia Andryszewski (Millbrook Press)

Terrorists and Terrorist Groups. Terrorism Library (series). Stephen Currie (Lucent)

Understanding September 11th: Answering Questions About the Attacks on America. Mitch Frank (Viking)

United We Stand: America's War Against Terrorism. Carole Marsh (Gallopade)

With Their Eyes: September 11th — the View from a High School at Ground Zero. Annie Thoms (editor) (HaperTempest)

Web Sites

http://abcnews.go.com/sections/2020/2020/2020/_010919_wtc_essay.html
Read how September 11, 2001 affected a New York City teenager.

www.fema.gov/hazards/terrorism/terrorf.shtm
Lists common-sense steps in response to different types of terrorism.

www.whitehouse.gov/news/releases/2002/03/20020312-5.html
Gives guidelines to the Department of Homeland Security.

www.writingproject.org/Resources/sept11.htm#parentsstudents
Scroll to bottom for a Youth Communication link to stories about tolerance, stereotyping, war, loss, and friendship.

www.awesomelibrary.org/Muslims.html
Discover information about Islam.